T0285250

Pavilion
An imprint of HarperCollinsPublishers Ltd
1 London Bridge Street
London SE1 9GF
www.harpercollins.co.uk

HarperCollinsPublishers
1st Floor, Watermarque Building
Ringsend Road Dublin 4
Ireland

10 9 8 7 6 5 4 3 2 1

First published in Great Britain by
Pavilion, an imprint of HarperCollinsPublishers Ltd 2022

Copyright © Linka Neumann, 2021 by Aschehoug. Published
in agreement with Northern Stories. (All rights reserved)

Linka Neumann asserts the moral right to be identified as
the author of this work.

A catalogue record for this book is available from the British
Library.

ISBN 978-1-911682-76-9

Design: Kitty Ensby
Photography:
@stineogjarlen / Stine Mette Fjerdingstad og Halvdan
Jarl Laugerud
Linka Neumann: pp. 12, 21, 55, 79, 81, 83, 92, 112, 114, 115, 120,
128, 139, 162
Sirikit Lockert: pp. 24, 32, 51, 53, 80, 87, 125, 168, 169
Kitty Ensby: pp. 101, 103, 107, 111
Mønsterdesign: Linka Neumann
Translated by: Elisabeth Stray Gausel

This book is produced from independently certified FSC™
paper to ensure responsible forest management.
For more information visit: www.harpercollins.co.uk/green

MIX
Paper from
responsible sources
FSC™ C007454

Printed and bound in China by RR Donnelley APS

All rights reserved. No part of this publication may be
reproduced, stored in a retrieval system, or transmitted,
in any form or by any means, electronic, mechanical,
photocopying, recording or otherwise, without the prior
permission of the publishers.

This book is sold subject to the condition that it shall not,
by way of trade or otherwise, be lent, re-sold, hired out or
otherwise circulated without the publisher's prior consent
in any form of binding or cover other than that in which it
is published and without a similar condition including this
condition being imposed on the subsequent purchaser.

LINKA NEUMANN

WILDERNESS
KNITS
FOR THE HOME

PAVILION

Contents

Preface   10
Practical info   12

LINKA BLANKET   17
WILDERNESS   25
   Blanket   34
   Cushion   36
KVITEBJØRN   39
   Tapestry   44
   Cushion   46
NENANA & KOBUK   49
   Nenana cushion   60
   Nenana tapestry   62
   Kobuk cushion   64
TAKOTNA   67
   Tapestry   72
   Cushion   74
ABENI & UMA   77
   Abeni tapestry   84
   Abeni cushion   86
   Uma cushion   88
TIPI   91
   Blanket   100
   Cushion   102
POLARBARN   105
   Blanket   106
   Single-sided blanket   110
ELISE'S tapestry   113
FØYKA cushion   121
KEIKO cushion   127
SOLSKOG cushion   133
SVARTULV cushion   138
TUNDRA cushion   141
LISTA cushion   147
ÅSGREINA blanket   153
POTHOLDERS   159

Hanging tapestries   168
Fringes   168
Assembling tapestries & blankets   169

Thank you   172

Preface

After the launch of my second book, the plan was to slow down
on the knitting for a while. My husband and I had bought an
old house in Åsgreina in Nannestad that was built in 1938, and
I wanted to spend time renovating and creating a home. I have
never been particularly interested in interior design, perhaps not
so strange since I have moved around a lot in recent years. I've
had a minimal amount of things, and my favourite possession is a
wooden pelican I bought in Mexico when I was 19 years old. Now I
have discovered how much fun it is to renovate and make the house
mine. And in step with the renovation, I felt like knitting things for
the new house!

When I finished knitting the first cushion, I thought it was so
nice that I just had to call my editor, Sirikit, to find out if she believed
in a wilderness interior knitting book. She did, and I just needed to
get started.

In many ways, it has been more joyful to work on this book
than the other two. The patterns are simpler, and I did not have
to calculate the number of stitches in many sizes. Instead, I have
enjoyed playing with my designs, putting them together in new ways
and giving them fresh uses.

Decorating with handmade knits is challenging and creative,
and I hope you will be inspired to knit for home and cottage. I'm
excited to see what colour combinations you choose!

Warm wishes,

Use leftover yarn

You will need a lot of yarn for the knitting projects in this book – for the cushions, but especially for blankets and tapestries. I love colours, and sometimes I cannot help myself adding a few rounds with one or two contrast colours as a little extra. Before buying yarn, I recommend you take stock of your yarn stash. Find your leftover yarn and sort it by colour tones: blue, red, etc. It does not matter if not everything fits the yarn types mentioned in this book. It also does not matter if the dye is different on the leftover yarn. This just gives a nice play of colours.

If the yarn is thinner, you can use it doubled. Doubled Léttlopi is equivalent to, for example, Álafosslopi. Doubled Vidde is equivalent to Blåne and Troll. Yarn alternative to Álafosslopi, Troll and Blåne: one strand Rauma Vams together with one strand Rauma Lamullgarn.

Where no colour codes
are given, leftover
yarn is used.

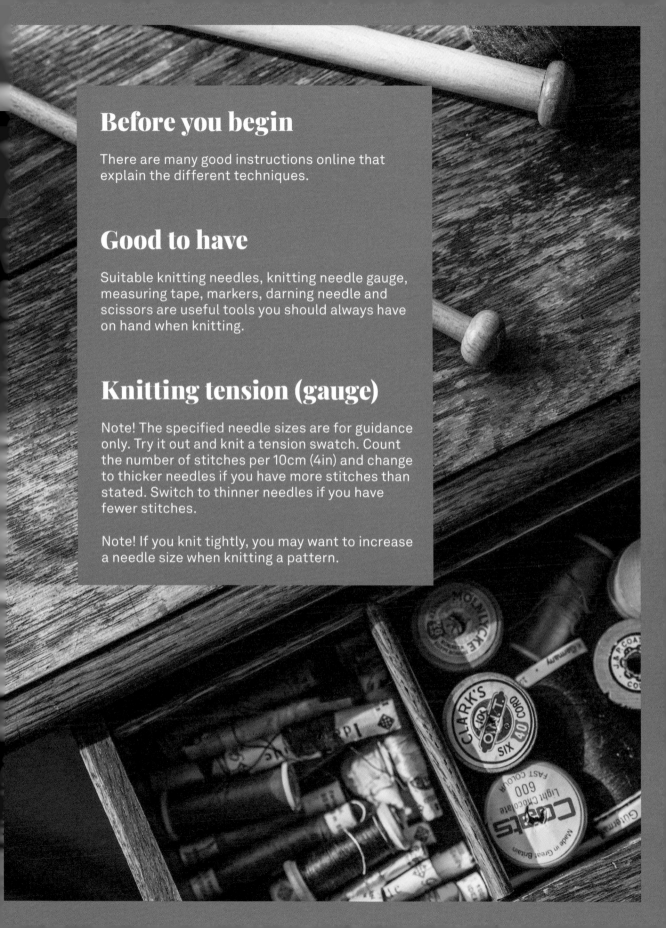

Before you begin

There are many good instructions online that explain the different techniques.

Good to have

Suitable knitting needles, knitting needle gauge, measuring tape, markers, darning needle and scissors are useful tools you should always have on hand when knitting.

Knitting tension (gauge)

Note! The specified needle sizes are for guidance only. Try it out and knit a tension swatch. Count the number of stitches per 10cm (4in) and change to thicker needles if you have more stitches than stated. Switch to thinner needles if you have fewer stitches.

Note! If you knit tightly, you may want to increase a needle size when knitting a pattern.

Linka blanket

I have enjoyed putting together favourite elements from my designs. The first Linka blanket I made is placed on my knitting chair, and I feel happy every time I look at it.

Álafosslopi and Léttlopi
Edge colour and fringes: Denim heather 800010
Beige tweed 809976
Black heather 800005
Teal heather 809967
Burnt orange 801236
Chocolate heather 800867
Léttlopi held double: Rust heather 19427
Ecru heather 809972
Arctic exposure 801232

Troll and Blåne
Edge colour and fringes: Troll Melert lys brun 02705
Troll Svart 02708
Troll Melert grå 02703
Blåne Burgunder 672104
Blåne Grønn 672126
Troll Melert oransje 027011
Troll Lys blåturkis 02760
Blåne Turkis 672106
Troll Melert mørk brun 02707

LINKA blanket

MEASUREMENTS

Length: approx. 124cm (48¾in) without fringes
Width: approx. 128cm (50½in)

TENSION (GAUGE)

10cm (4in) on 7mm (US 10½/11) needle = 12 sts

YARN

Álafosslopi, Blåne or Troll from Hillesvåg Ullvarefabrikk, or Rauma Vams and one strand Lamullgarn

AMOUNT OF YARN

Edge and fringes: 400g (14oz)

Base colour: 300g (10½oz)

Pattern colour 1: 200g (7oz)

Pattern colour 2: 200g (7oz)

Pattern colour 3: 100g (3½oz)

Pattern colour 4: 100g (3½oz)

Pattern colour 5: 100g (3½oz)

Pattern colour 6: 100g (3½oz)

Pattern colour 7: 100g (3½oz)

TOOLS

6mm & 7mm (US 10 & 10½/11) 80cm or 100cm (32in or 40in) circular needles
Crochet hook for the fringes
Sewing machine

Note! In some places on the back there will be long floats, make sure to catch them as you work.

With 6mm (US 10) needle and edge colour, cast on 144 sts. Work garter st in rows for 6cm (2¼in). Cast on 5 sts on right needle for steek sts (these are not included in the number of sts and are worked purl at all times). Change to 7mm (US 10½/11) needle and continue working stocking (stockinette) st in the round. Knit charts A, B, C, and D.

When you have finished the charts, work 1 round in the edge colour and cast (bind) off the steek sts. Change to 6mm (US 10) needle and work rows of garter st for 6cm (2¼in). Cast (bind) off.

In the steek sts, sew two double seams with a sewing machine. You can either cut before picking up sts for the edge, or you can wait until both edges have been knitted. Pick up sts with 6mm (US 10) needle in edge colour along the right side of the blanket (pick up 2 sts, skip 1 st, rep to end). When you have picked up all the sts on the needle, run a contrasting strand of yarn through all the sts. This makes it easier to pick up sts for binding to cover the cut edge later on. Work garter st in rows for 4cm (1½in). Cast (bind) off.

Repeat on the left side.

Binding: Now that there is a strand of contrasting yarn through the sts, it is easy to see which sts to pick up for the binding. Using 6mm (US 10) needle and base colour, pick up sts where the contrasting yarn is (pick up 2 sts, skip 1 st, rep to end) and remove the strand. Work 4 rows stocking (stockinette) st. Cast (bind) off and sew the binding loosely over the cut edge. Do the same on the other side. Alternatively, you can hide the cut edge by sewing on a ribbon.

Make fringes using the edge colour (or the colour you prefer). See page 168 for details.
Weave in ends. Rinse the blanket and stretch it into shape. Let it dry flat.

Chart A

53
51
49
47
45
43
41
39
37
35
33
31
29
27
25
23
21
19
17
15
13
11
9
7
5
3
1

16 14 12 10 8 6 4 2 ▲
Start here

Chart B

76
74
72
70
68
66
64
62
60
58
56
54

36 34 32 30 28 26 24 22 20 18 16 14 12 10 8 6 4 2 ▲
Start here

Chart C

118
116
114
112
110
108
106
104
102
100
98
96
94
92
90
88
86
84
82
80
78

16 14 12 10 8 6 4 2 ▲
Start here

Chart D

169
167
165
163
161
159
157
155
153
151
149
147
145
143
141
139
137
135
133
131
129
127
125
123
121
119

48 46 44 42 40 38 36 34 32 30 28 26 24 22 20 18 16 14 12 10 8 6 4 2 ▲
Start here

Wilderness
blanket and cushion

My dogs, Obelix and Sakura, love to lie on my wool sweaters, especially those knitted in Álafosslopi. Therefore, I have wanted to knit a blanket for them for a long time. The blanket comes in two sizes. Underneath the largest blanket there is room for both dog and owner, while the smallest fits on the dog's favourite chair or in a dog bed.

Álafosslopi
Dusk red 801238
Beige tweed 809976
Chocolate heather 800867
Navy 800118
Arctic exposure 801232
Golden heather 809964

Álafosslopi
Ray of light 801235
Midnight blue 800709
Wheat heather 809973
Arctic exposure 801232
Sheep sorrel 801237

Álafosslopi
Teal heather 809967
Golden heather 809964
Burnt orange 801236
Arctic exposure 801232

Blåne and Troll
Troll Jaktgrønn 02732
Troll Melert oransje 027011
Blåne Cognac 672103
Troll Ubleket hvit 02702

Leftover Álafosslopi yarn
Light grey tweed 809974/Light ash heather 800054
Chocolate heather 800867
Denim heather 800010
Highland green 801230
Oatmeal heather 800085

WILDERNESS blanket

MEASUREMENTS

Size: S/M(L/XL)
Length: approx. 118(155)cm (46½(61)in)
without fringes
Width: approx. 107(127)cm (42(50)in)

TENSION (GAUGE)

10cm (4in) on 6mm (US 10) needle = 13 sts

YARN

Álafosslopi, Blåne or Troll from Hillesvåg
Ullvarefabrikk, or Rauma Vams and one
strand Lamullgarn

AMOUNT OF YARN

Base colour: 500(800)g
(17½(28¼)oz)

Pattern colour 1: 400(500)g
(14(17½)oz)

Pattern colour 2: 200(200)g
(7(7)oz)

Pattern colour 3: 100(100)g
(3½(3½)oz)

Pattern colour 4: 100(100)g
(3½(3½)oz)

Pattern colour 5: 100(100)g
(3½(3½)oz)

TOOLS

5mm & 6mm (US 8 & 10) 80cm or 100cm
(32in or 40in) circular needles
Crochet hook for the fringes
Sewing machine

With 5mm (US 8) needle and pattern colour 1, cast
on 144(192) sts. Work garter st in rows for 4cm (1½in).
Cast on 5 sts on right needle for steek sts (these are
not included in the number of sts and are worked
purl at all times). Change to 6mm (US 10) needle and
cont working in stocking (stockinette) st in the round.
Knit chart A. Continue knitting in base colour 20(30)
cm (8(11¾)in). Knit chart B. Continue knitting in base
colour for 20(30)cm (8(11¾)in) before knitting chart C.
Cast (bind) off the steek sts. Change to 5mm (US 8)
needle and work rows of garter st for 4cm (1½in). Cast
(bind) off. On either side of the steek sts, sew two
double seams with a sewing machine. You can either
cut before picking up sts for the edge, or you can wait
until both edges have been knitted. Pick up sts with
5mm (US 8) needle in pattern colour 1 along the right
side of the blanket (pick up 2 sts, skip 1 st, rep to end).
When you have picked up all the sts on the needle, run
a strand of contrasting yarn through all the sts. This
makes it easier to pick up sts for the binding to cover
the cut edge later on. Work garter st in rows for 4cm
(1½in). Cast (bind) off. Repeat on the left side.

Binding: Now that there is a strand of contrasting
yarn through the sts, it is easy to see which sts to
pick up for the binding. Using 6mm (US 10) needle and
base colour, pick up sts where the contrasting yarn is
(pick up 2, skip 1, rep to end) and remove the strand.
Work 4 rows stocking (stockinette) sts. Cast (bind) off
and sew the binding loosely over the cut edge. Do the
same on the other side. Alternatively, you can hide
the cut edge by sewing on a ribbon.

Make fringes using pattern colour 1 and 3 (or the
colours you prefer). See page 168 for details.
Weave in ends. Rinse the blanket and stretch it into
shape. Let it dry flat.

> Note! In some places on the back there
> will be long floats, make sure to catch
> them as you work.

Chart A

Chart C

Chart B

WILDERNESS cushion

MEASUREMENTS

50x50cm (19¾x19¾in)

TENSION (GAUGE)

10cm (4in) on 6mm (US 10) needle = 13 sts

YARN

Álafosslopi, Blåne or Troll from Hillesvåg Ullvarefabrikk, or Rauma Vams and one strand Lamullgarn

AMOUNT OF YARN

Base colour: Troll/Blåne 200g (7oz) or Álafosslopi 300g (10½oz)

Pattern colour 1: 100g (3½oz)

Pattern colour 2: 100g (3½oz)

Pattern colour 3: 100g (3½oz)

KNITTING NEEDLES

6mm (US 10) 80cm (32in) circular needle
5mm (US 8) 80cm (32in) circular needle (for removable cushion cover)

BUTTONS

6 22mm (1in) buttons (for removable cushion cover)

With 6mm (US 10) needle and base colour, cast on 128 sts, and place a marker at the beginning of the needle and after 64 sts (one marker on each side). Work the chart. The whole cushion is knitted in stocking (stockinette) st in the round. When you have finished the chart, sew together with Kitchener stitch.

Weave in ends. Rinse the cushion and stretch it into shape. Let it dry flat. Fill the cushion (e.g. 50x50cm (19¾x19¾in) inner cushion from Ikea). Sew together the other side.

Removable cushion cover:
If you would like a removable cushion cover, cast (bind) off the first 64 sts (=backside). Change to 5mm (US 8) needle and work the remaining 64 sts in garter st rows for 2cm (¾in). Make 6 buttonholes (knit 2 sts together, yarn over) evenly spaced. Continue for 2cm (¾in) and cast (bind) off. Sew buttons on backside.

> Note! In some places on the back there will be long floats, make sure to catch them as you work.

Álafosslopi and Léttlopi
Black tweed 809975
Beige tweed 809976
Teal heather 809967
Chocolate heather 800867
Léttlopi held double: Rust heather 19427
Arctic exposure 801232
Light denim heather 800008
Léttlopi held double: Glacier blue heather 11404

Kvitebjørn
tapestry and cushion

I never get bored of the Kvitebjørn design, and in this book you will find a tapestry and a cushion. You can choose between both a medium and a large tapestry. The design is also an element of the Linka blanket.

I love using colours, and in this pattern there are eight colours. If you think there are too many, you can make a simpler variation with fewer colours, for example, by using a single colour behind the polar bears.

Álafosslopi
Chocolate heather 800867
Arctic exposure 801232
Burnt orange 801236
Dark olive 809987
Teal heather 809967
Light beige heather 800086
Wheat heather 809973
Amber heather 809971

Álafosslopi and Léttlopi
White 800051
Light indigo 809958
Light denim heather 800008
Léttlopi held double: Apricot 11704
Léttlopi held double: Garnet red heather 11409
Léttlopi held double: Glacier blue heather 11404
Léttlopi held double: Lagoon heather 19423
Léttlopi held double: Lapis blue heather 11403

Álafosslopi
White 800051
Fuchsia heather 809969
Arctic exposure 801232
Golden heather 809964
Teal heather 809967
Light indigo 809958
Space blue 801233
Midnight blue 800709

Álafosslopi
Light grey tweed 809974
Golden heather 809964
Chocolate heather 800867
Amber heather 809971
Burnt orange 801236
Arctic exposure 801232
Black tweed 809975
Teal heather 809967

TIPI CUSHION (p.102)

SVARTULV CUSHION (p.138)
Blåne
Cognac 672103
Olivengrønn 672118

ÅSGREINA BLANKET (p.153)

KVITEBJØRN tapestry

MEASUREMENTS

Size: M(L)
Height: approx. 75cm (29½in) without fringe
Width: approx. 61cm(116)cm (24(45¾)in)

TENSION (GAUGE)

10cm (4in) on 6mm (US 10) needle = 13 sts

YARN

Álafosslopi, Blåne or Troll from Hillesvåg Ullvarefabrikk, or Rauma Vams and one strand Lamullgarn

AMOUNT OF YARN

☐ Base colour: 300(400)g (10½(14)oz)

◼ Pattern colour 1: 100g (3½oz)

◼ Pattern colour 2: 100g (3½oz)

◼ Pattern colour 3: 100g (3½oz)

◼ Pattern colour 4: 100g (3½oz)

◼ Pattern colour 5: 100g (3½oz)

◼ Pattern colour 6: 100g (3½oz)

◼ Pattern colour 7: 100g (3½oz)

TOOLS

6mm (US 10) 80cm (32in) circular needle
Crochet hook for the fringe
Wooden stick for hanging
Sewing machine

With 6mm (US 10) needle and base colour, cast on 72(144) sts. Work garter st in rows for 4cm (1½in). Cast on 5 sts on right needle for steek sts (these sts are not included in the number of sts and are worked purl at all times). Continue in stocking (stockinette) st in the round. Knit chart. When the chart is completed, work garter st in base colour for 12cm (4¾in) (this will become the rod sleeve). Cast (bind) off.

In the steek sts, sew two double seams with a sewing machine. You can either cut before picking up sts for the edge, or you can wait until both edges have been knitted. Pick up sts in base colour along the right edge of the tapestry (pick up 2 sts, skip 1 st, rep to end). Work garter st rows for 4cm (1½in). Cast (bind) off. Repeat on the left side.
Trim the cut edges. Do not knit binding to hide the cut edge, as it will appear on the front of the tapestry. You can hide the cut edge by sewing on a ribbon.

Fold over the rod sleeve and sew it to the tapestry. Insert the wooden stick. See page 168 for details.

Make fringe in the base colour. See page 168. Weave in ends. Rinse the tapestry and stretch it into shape. Let it dry flat.

> Note! In some places on the back there will be long floats, make sure to catch them as you work.

KVITEBJØRN cushion

MEASUREMENTS

50x50cm (19¾x19¾in)

TENSION (GAUGE)

10cm (4in) on 6mm (US 10) needle = 13 sts

YARN

Álafosslopi, Blåne or Troll from Hillesvåg Ullvarefabrikk, or Rauma Vams and one strand Lamullgarn

AMOUNT OF YARN

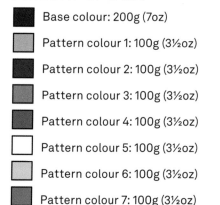

Base colour: 200g (7oz)

Pattern colour 1: 100g (3½oz)

Pattern colour 2: 100g (3½oz)

Pattern colour 3: 100g (3½oz)

Pattern colour 4: 100g (3½oz)

Pattern colour 5: 100g (3½oz)

Pattern colour 6: 100g (3½oz)

Pattern colour 7: 100g (3½oz)

KNITTING NEEDLES

6mm (US 10) 80cm (32in) circular needle
5mm (US 8) 80cm (40in) circular needle
(for removable cushion cover)

BUTTONS

6 22mm (1in) buttons (for removable cushion cover)

With 6mm (US 10) needle and base colour, cast on 132 sts. Place a marker at the beginning of the needle and after 66 sts (one marker on each side). Work the chart. The whole cushion is knitted in stocking (stockinette) st in the round. When you have finished the chart, sew together with Kitchener stitch.

Weave in ends. Rinse the cushion and stretch it into shape. Let it dry flat. Fill the cushion (e.g. 50x50cm (19¾x19¾in) inner cushion from Ikea). Sew together the other side.

Removable cushion cover:
If you would like a removable cushion cover, cast (bind) off the first 66 sts (=backside). Change to 5mm (US 8) needle and work the remaining 66 sts in garter st rows for 2cm (¾in). Make 6 buttonholes (knit 2 sts together, yarn over) evenly spaced. Continue for 2cm (¾in) and cast (bind) off. Sew buttons on backside.

> Note! In some places on the back there will be long floats, make sure to catch them as you work.

Nenana & Kobuk
cushions and tapestry

Nenana and Kobuk were the first cushions I designed, and are perhaps the most classic patterns in this book. Kobuk and Nenana are rivers in Alaska, but also the names of two dogs from Helge Ingstad's kennel who I spent a lot of time with growing up. As you can see in the pictures, there are endless possibilities for colour combinations, and the wonderful thing is that all the cushions are just as nice.

Kobuk has a beautiful pattern that fits perfectly on both sides of the cushion.

Troll
Melert lys brun 02705
Melert brun 02706
Jaktgrønn 02732
Blek rosa 02747
Brun 02715
Oker 02713

Troll
Mørk kamel 02714
Oker 02713
Blek rosa 02747
Jaktgrønn 02732
Melert brun 02706

ÅSGREINA BLANKET (p.153)

Blåne
Rosa 672110
Mørk brun 672116
Lys brun 672102
Rødgul 672122
Naturgrå 672115

Álafosslopi
Light ash heather 800054
Burnt orange 801236
Chocolate heather 800867
Denim heather 800010
Oatmeal heather 800085
Light denim heather 800008

Álafosslopi
Light ash heather 800054
Chocolate heather 800867
Burnt orange 801236
Denim heather 800010
Oatmeal heather 800085

Álafosslopi and Léttlopi
Ecru heather 809972
Arctic exposure 801232
Chocolate heather 800867
Burnt orange 801236
Teal heather 809967
Léttlopi held double: Rust heather 19427

Álafosslopi
Wheat heather 809973
Chocolate heather 800867
Burnt orange 801236
Teal heather 809967
Amber heather 809971

Álafosslopi
Beige tweed 809976
Dark olive 809987
Arctic exposure 801232
Dusk red 801238
Navy 800118
Golden heather 809964

TUNDRA CUSHION (p.141)

UMA CUSHION (p.88)

Troll and Blåne
Troll Melert oransje 027011
Troll Jaktgrønn 02732
Troll Melert lys turkis 027303
Blåne Støvet rosa 672137
Troll Halvbleket hvit 02754
Blåne Petrol 672105

NENANA cushion

MEASUREMENTS
50x50cm (19¾x19¾in)

TENSION (GAUGE)
10cm (4in) on 6mm (US 10) needle = 13 sts

YARN
Álafosslopi, Blåne or Troll from Hillesvåg Ullvarefabrikk, or Rauma Vams and one strand Lamullgarn

AMOUNT OF YARN
Base colour: 200g (7oz)

Pattern colour 1: 100g (3½oz)

Pattern colour 2: 100g (3½oz)

Pattern colour 3: 100g (3½oz)

Pattern colour 4: 100g (3½oz)

Pattern colour 5: 100g (3½oz)

KNITTING NEEDLES
6mm (US 10) 80cm (32in) circular needle
5mm (US 8) 80cm (32in) circular needle (for removable cushion cover)

BUTTONS
6 22mm (1in) buttons (for removable cushion cover)

With 6mm (US 10) needle and base colour, cast on 132 sts, and place a marker at the beginning of the needle and after 66 sts (one marker on each side). Work the chart. The cushion is knitted in stocking (stockinette) st in the round. When you have finished the chart, sew together with Kitchener stitch.

Weave in ends. Rinse the cushion and stretch it into shape. Let it dry flat. Fill the cushion (e.g. 50x50cm (19¾x19¾in) inner cushion from Ikea). Sew together the other side.

Removable cushion cover:
If you would like a removable cushion cover, cast (bind) off the first 66 sts (=backside). Change to 5mm (US 8) needle and work the remaining 66 sts in garter st rows for 2cm (¾in). Make 6 buttonholes (knit 2 sts together, yarn over) evenly spaced. Continue for 2cm (¾in) and cast (bind) off. Sew buttons on backside.

Note! In some places on the back there will be long floats, make sure to catch them as you work.

NENANA tapestry

MEASUREMENTS

Size: M(L)
Height: approx. 77cm (30¼in) without fringe
Width: approx. 56(107)cm (22(42)in)

TENSION (GAUGE)

10cm (4in) on 6mm (US 10) needle = 13 sts

YARN

Álafosslopi, Blåne or Troll from Hillesvåg Ullvarefabrikk, or Rauma Vams and one strand Lamullgarn

AMOUNT OF YARN

Base colour: 200(400)g (7(14)oz)

Pattern colour 1: 100(100)g (3½oz)

Pattern colour 2: 100(100)g (3½oz)

Pattern colour 3: 100(100)g (3½oz)

Pattern colour 4: 100(100)g (3½oz)

Pattern colour 5: 100(100)g (3½oz)

TOOLS

6mm (US 10) 80cm (32in) circular needle
Crochet hook for the fringe
Wooden stick for hanging
Sewing machine

With 6mm (US 10) needle and base colour, cast on 66(132) sts. Work garter st rows for 3cm (1¼in). Cast on 5 sts on right needle for steek sts (these sts are not included in the number of sts and are worked purl at all times). Continue in stocking (stockinette) st in the round. Work the chart. When the chart is completed, work garter st in base colour for 12cm (4¾in) (this will become the rod sleeve). Cast (bind) off.

In the steek stitches, sew two double seams with a sewing machine. You can either cut before picking up sts for the edge, or you can wait until both edges have been knitted. Pick up sts in base colour along the right edge of the tapestry (pick up 2 sts, skip 1 st, rep to end). Work garter st rows for 3cm (1¼in). Cast (bind) off. Repeat the same on the left side. Trim the cut edges.
Do not knit binding to hide the cut edge, as it will appear on the front of the tapestry. You can hide the cut edge by sewing on a ribbon.

Fringe: Make fringe in the base colour. See page 168 for details. Weave in ends. Rinse the tapestry and stretch it into shape. Let it dry flat.

Fold over the rod sleeve and sew it to the tapestry. Insert the wooden stick. See page 168 for details.

> Note! In some places on the back there will be long floats, make sure to catch them as you work.

KOBUK cushion

MEASUREMENTS
50x50cm (19¾x19¾cm)

TENSION (GAUGE)
10cm (4in) on 6mm (US 10) needle = 13 sts

YARN
Álafosslopi, Blåne or Troll from Hillesvåg Ullvarefabrikk, or Rauma Vams and one strand Lamullgarn

AMOUNT OF YARN

Base colour: 200g (7oz)

Pattern colour 1: 100g (3½oz)

Pattern colour 2: 100g (3½oz)

Pattern colour 3: 100g (3½oz)

Pattern colour 4: 100g (3½oz)

KNITTING NEEDLES
6mm (US 10) 80cm (32in) circular needle
5mm (US 8) 80cm (32in) circular needle (for removable cushion cover)

BUTTONS
6 22mm (1in) buttons (for removable cushion cover)

With 6mm (US 10) needle and pattern colour 1, cast on 132 sts and place a marker at the beginning of the needle and after 66 sts (one marker on each side). Work the chart. The cushion is knitted in stocking (stockinette) st in the round. When you have finished the chart, sew together with Kitchener stitch.

Weave in ends. Rinse the cushion and stretch it into shape. Let it dry flat. Fill the cushion (e.g. 50x50cm (19¾x19¾cm) inner cushion from Ikea). Sew together the other side.

Removable cushion cover:
If you would like a removable cushion cover, cast (bind) off the first 66 sts (=backside). Change to 5mm (US 8) needle and work the remaining 66 sts in garter st rows for 2cm (¾in). Make 6 buttonholes (knit 2 sts together, yarn over) evenly spaced. Continue for 2cm (¾in) and cast (bind) off. Sew buttons on backside.

Note! In some places on the back there will be long floats, make sure to catch them as you work.

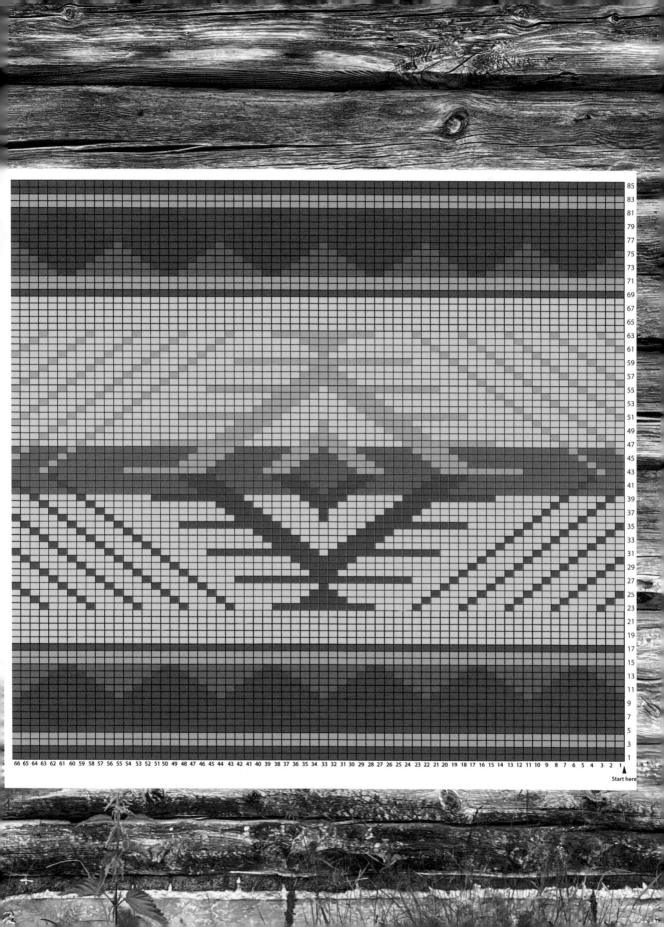

Takotna
tapestry and cushion

Tapestries are not something you see so often in
modern homes, but I think they create a nice, cosy
atmosphere in a room. They have a long tradition
in Norway and were used as bedspreads. Skin rugs
were sewn on and they were hung up for decoration
and insulation.

Álafosslopi
Ray of light 801235
Teal heather 809967
Sheep sorrel 801237
Arctic exposure 801232
Amber heather 809971

Álafosslopi
Space blue 801233
Burnt orange 801236
Amber heather 809971
Cypress green heather 809966
Golden heather 809964

Blåne and Troll
Blåne Petrol 672105
Troll Oker 02713
Blåne Cognac 672103
Troll Mørk kamel 02714
Troll Melert mørk brun 02707

KEIKO CUSHION (p.127)

TIPI CUSHION (p.102)

NENANA CUSHION (p.60)

TAKOTNA CUSHION (p.74)

TAKOTNA tapestry

MEASUREMENTS

Size: M(L)
Height: approx. 77cm (30¼in) without fringes
Width: approx. 61(116)cm (24(45¾)in)

TENSION (GAUGE)

10cm (4in) on 6mm (US 10) needle = 13 sts

YARN

Álafosslopi, Blåne or Troll from Hillesvåg Ullvarefabrikk, or Rauma Vams and one strand Lamullgarn

AMOUNT OF YARN

Base colour: 300(400)g (10½(14)oz)

Pattern colour 1: 100(100)g (3½(3½)oz)

Pattern colour 2: 100(100)g (3½(3½)oz)

Pattern colour 3: 100(200)g (3½(7)oz)

Pattern colour 4: 100(200)g (3½(7)oz)

TOOLS

6mm (US 10) 60(80)cm (24(32)in) circular needle
Crochet hook for the fringe
Wooden stick for hanging
Sewing machine

With 6mm (US 10) needle and base colour, cast on 72(144) sts. Work garter st rows for 4cm (1½in). Cast on 5 sts on right needle for steek sts (these sts are not included in the number of sts and are worked the purl at all times). From here, work stocking (stockinette) st in the round. Work the chart. When the chart is completed, work garter st in base colour for 12cm (4¾in) (this will become the rod sleeve). Cast (bind) off.

In the steek sts, sew two double seams with a sewing machine. You can either cut before picking up sts for the edge, or you can wait until both edges have been knitted. Pick up sts in base colour along the right edge of the tapestry (pick up 2 sts, skip 1 st, rep to end). Work garter st rows for 3cm (1¼in). Cast (bind) off. Repeat on the left side.

Trim the cut edges. Do not knit binding to hide the cut edge, as it will appear on the front of the tapestry. You can hide the cut edge by sewing on a ribbon.

Fringe: Make fringe in the base colour. See page 168 for details. Weave in ends. Rinse the tapestry and stretch it into shape. Let it dry flat.

Fold over the rod sleeve and sew it to the tapestry. Insert the wooden stick. See page 168 for details.

> Note! In some places on the back there will be long floats, make sure to catch them as you work.

TAKOTNA cushion

MEASUREMENTS
50x50cm (19¾x19¾in)

TENSION (GAUGE)
10cm (4in) on 5.5mm (US 9) needle
= 14 sts

YARN
Álafosslopi, Blåne or Troll from Hillesvåg
Ullvarefabrikk, or Rauma Vams and one
strand Lamullgarn

AMOUNT OF YARN
Base colour: 200g (7oz)

Pattern colour 1: 100g (3½oz)

Pattern colour 2: 100g (3½oz)

Pattern colour 3: 100g (3½oz)

Pattern colour 4: 100g (3½oz)

KNITTING NEEDLES
5.5mm (US 9) 80cm (32in) circular needle
4.5mm (US 7) 80cm (32in) circular needle
(for removable cushion cover)

BUTTONS
6 22mm (1in) buttons (for removable
cushion cover)

With 5.5mm (US 9) needle and base colour, cast on
144 sts and place a marker at the beginning of the
needle and after 72 sts (one marker on each side).
Work the chart. The cushion is knitted in stocking
(stockinette) st in the round. When you have finished
the chart, sew together with Kitchener stitch.

Weave in ends. Rinse the cushion and stretch it into
shape. Let it dry flat. Fill the cushion (e.g. 50x50cm
(19¾x19¾in) inner cushion from Ikea). Sew together
the other side.

Removable cushion cover:
If you would like a removable cushion cover, cast
(bind) off the first 72 sts (=backside). Change to
4.5mm (US 7) needle and work the remaining 72 sts
in garter st rows for 2cm (¾in). Make 6 buttonholes
(knit 2 sts together, yarn over) evenly spaced.
Continue for 2cm (¾in) and cast (bind) off. Sew
buttons on backside.

> Note! In some places on the back
> there will be long floats, make sure
> to catch them as you work.

Troll
Marineblå 02724
Kobberrød 02716
Oker 02713
Brun 02715
Mørk kamel 02714

UMA CUSHION (p.88)

Troll and Blåne
Blåne Cognac 672103
Troll Melert oransje 027011
Troll Svart 02708
Troll Ubleket hvit 02702

Abeni & Uma
tapestry and cushions

The Abeni and Uma designs are inspired by African patterns. I have always liked the combination of bold patterns and clear and strong colours. I was not so bold that I dared to go for the most vibrant colours. Instead I toned it down so that the cushions would fit into our living room and the cabin.

Álafosslopi
Black heather 800005
Golden heather 809964
Denim heather 800010
Burnt orange 801236

Álafosslopi
Light ash heather 800054
Golden heather 809964
Chocolate heather 800867
Denim heather 800010

Rauma Vams and one strand Lamullgarn
Melon 113 and Oransje-01062
Mørk blå 067 and Bondeblå-01068
Vinrød 35 and Mørk rød-01035
Brun 106 and Brun-01034
Kamelbrun 104 and Oker-01036
Jadegrønn 107 and Jadegrønn-01054

Rauma Vams and one strand Lamullgarn
Mørk blå 067 and Bondeblå-01068
Melon 113 and Oransje-01062
Jadegrønn 107 and Jadegrønn-01054
Kobberrød 105 and Mørk rød-01035

NENANA CUSHION (p.60)

ABENI tapestry

MEASUREMENTS

Height: approx. 91cm (35¾in) without fringe
Width: approx. 47cm (18½in)

TENSION (GAUGE)

10cm (4in) on 6mm (US 10) needle = 13 sts

YARN

Álafosslopi, Blåne or Troll from Hillesvåg Ullvarefabrikk, or Rauma Vams and one strand Lamullgarn

AMOUNT OF YARN

◼ Edge colour: 300g (10½oz)

◻ Pattern colour 1: 200g (7oz)

◼ Pattern colour 2: 100g (3½oz)

◼ Pattern colour 3: 100g (3½oz)

TOOLS

6mm (US 10) 60cm (24in) circular needle
Crochet hook for the fringe
Wooden stick for hanging
Sewing machine

With 6mm (US 10) needle and edge colour, cast on 100 sts. Work garter st rows for 3cm (1¼in). Cast on 5 sts on right needle for steek sts (these sts are not included in the number of sts and are worked purl at all times). From here, work stocking (stockinette) st in the round. Work the chart. When the chart is completed, cast (bind) off the steek sts and work garter st rows for 3cm (1¼in). Cast (bind) off.

In the steek sts, sew two double seams with a sewing machine. You can either cut before picking up sts for the edge, or you can wait until both edges have been knitted. Pick up sts in the edge colour along what is now the bottom edge of the tapestry (pick up 2 sts, skip 1 st, rep to end). Work garter st rows for 4cm (1½in). Cast (bind) off. Pick up sts in what is now the top of the tapestry, and work stocking (stockinette) st rows for 12cm (4¾in) (this will become the rod sleeve). Cast (bind) off.

Trim the cut edges. Do not knit binding to hide the cut edge, as it will appear on the front of the tapestry. You can hide the cut edge by sewing on a ribbon.

Make fringe in the edge colour. See page 168 for details. Weave in ends. Rinse the tapestry and stretch it into shape. Let it dry flat.

Fold over the rod sleeve and sew it to the tapestry. Insert the wooden stick. See page 168 for details.

> Note! In some places on the back there will be long floats, make sure to catch them as you work.

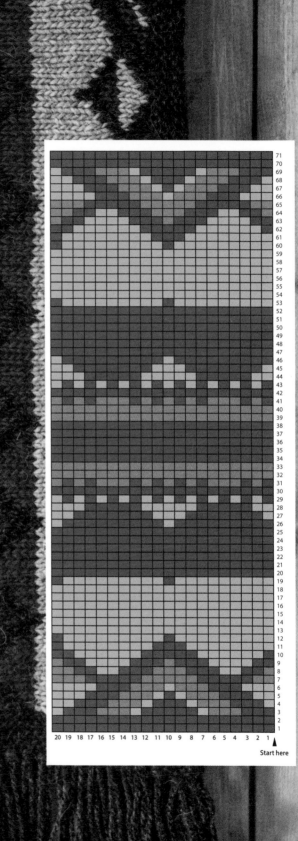

Álafosslopi and Léttlopi
Black heather 800005
Golden heather 809964
Garden green 801231
Léttlopi held double: Brick heather 19431

ABENI cushion

MEASUREMENTS
50x50cm (19¾x19¾in)

TENSION (GAUGE)
10cm (4in) on 5.5mm (US 9) needle
= 14 sts

YARN
Álafosslopi, Blåne or Troll from Hillesvåg
Ullvarefabrikk, or Rauma Vams and one
strand Lamullgarn

AMOUNT OF YARN

Base colour: 300g (10½oz)

Pattern colour 1: 200g (7oz)

Pattern colour 2: 100g (3½oz)

Pattern colour 3: 100g (3½oz)

KNITTING NEEDLES
5.5mm (US 9) 80cm (32in) circular needle
4.5mm (US 7) 80cm (32in) circular needle
(for removable cushion cover)

BUTTONS
6 22mm (1in) buttons (for removable
cushion cover)

With 5.5mm (US 9) needle and base colour, cast on
140 sts and place a marker at the beginning of the
needle and after 70 sts (one marker on each side).
Work the chart. The cushion is knitted in stocking
(stockinette) st in the round. When you have finished
the chart, sew together with Kitchener stitch.

Weave in ends. Rinse the cushion and stretch it into
shape. Let it dry flat. Fill the cushion (e.g. 50x50cm
(19¾x19¾in) inner cushion from Ikea). Sew together
the other side.

Removable cushion cover:
If you would like a removable cushion cover, cast
(bind) off the first 70 sts (=backside). Change to
4.5mm (US 7) needle and work the remaining 70 sts
in garter st rows for 2cm (¾in). Make 6 buttonholes
(knit 2 sts together, yarn over) evenly spaced.
Continue for 2cm (¾in) and cast (bind) off. Sew
buttons on backside.

> Note! In some places on the back
> there will be long floats, make sure
> to catch them as you work.

UMA cushion

MEASUREMENTS
50x50cm (19¾x19¾in)

TENSION (GAUGE)
10cm (4in) on 6mm (US 10) needle = 13 sts

YARN
Álafosslopi, Blåne or Troll from Hillesvåg Ullvarefabrikk, or Rauma Vams and one strand Lamullgarn

AMOUNT OF YARN
- Pattern colour 1: 200g (7oz)
- Pattern colour 2: 200g (7oz)
- Pattern colour 3: 100g (3½oz)
- Pattern colour 4: 100g (3½oz)

KNITTING NEEDLES
6mm (US 10) 80cm (32in) circular needle
5mm (US 8) 80cm (32in) circular needle
(for removable cushion cover)

BUTTONS
6 22mm (1in) buttons (for removable cushion cover)

With 6mm (US 10) needle and pattern colour 1, cast on 132 sts. Place a marker at the beginning of the needle and after 66 sts (one marker on each side). Work the chart. The cushion is knitted in stocking (stockinette) st in the round. When you have finished the chart, sew together with Kitchener stitch.

Weave in ends. Rinse the cushion and stretch it into shape. Let it dry flat. Fill the cushion (e.g. 50x50cm (19¾x19¾in) inner cushion from Ikea). Sew together the other side.

Removable cushion cover:
If you would like a removable cushion cover, cast (bind) off the first 66 sts (=backside). Change to 5mm (US 8) needle and work the remaining 66 sts in garter st rows for 2cm (¾in). Make 6 buttonholes (knit 2 sts together, yarn over) evenly spaced. Continue for 2cm (¾in) and cast (bind) off. Sew buttons on backside.

Álafosslopi
Amber heather 809971
Teal Heather 809967
Black tweed 809975
Ecru heather 809972

Blåne and Troll
Blåne Ren grønn 672141
Blåne Burgunder 672104
Blåne Marineblå 672133
Troll Bonderød 02746
Troll Oker 02713

Tipi
blanket and cushion

The lavvu tents remind me of my childhood. I remember rainy days when we sat indoors and watched the Moomins. I loved the Moomin universe and especially Snufkin. I thought it looked so harmonious when Snufkin was sitting outside his tent fishing.

Rauma Vams and Lamullgarn
Grå melert 13 and Lys grå melert-01012
Skoggrønn 87 and Mørk grønn-01094
Kobberrød 105 and Mørk rød-01035
Jadegrønn 107 and Jadegrønn-01054
Mørk brun melert 64 and Brun-01034

Troll
Lys gul 02709
Blek rosa 02747
Lyseblå 02725
Lillarosa 02721
Lys blåturkis 02780

Troll
Mørk kamel 02714
Mosegrønn 02728
Brun 02715
Oker 02713
Melert rustrød 027308

TIPI blanket

MEASUREMENTS

Length: approx. 120cm (47¼in)
Width: approx. 165cm (65in) without fringes

TENSION (GAUGE)

10cm (4in) on 6mm (US 10) needle = 13 sts

YARN

Álafosslopi, Blåne or Troll from Hillesvåg Ullvarefabrikk, or Rauma Vams and one strand Lamullgarn

AMOUNT OF YARN

▢ Base colour: 700g (24½oz)

▢ Pattern colour 1: 400g (14oz)

▢ Pattern colour 2: 100g (3½oz)

▢ Pattern colour 3: 100g (3½oz)

▢ Pattern colour 4: 300g (10½oz)

TOOLS

5mm & 6mm (US 8 &10) 80cm or 100cm (32in or 40in) circular needles
Crochet hook for the fringes
Sewing machine

Note! In some places on the back there will be long floats, make sure to catch them as you work.

With 5mm (US 8) needle and pattern colour 1, cast on 200 sts. Work garter st rows for 4cm (1½in). Cast on 5 sts on right needle for steek sts (these sts are not included in the number of sts and are worked purl at all times). From here, work stocking (stockinette) st in the round. Work chart A. Continue knitting in base colour until work is 34cm (13½in), and then begin knitting chart B. Continue knitting in base colour so the two solid-coloured fields are equal (approx. 23cm (9in)). Finish by knitting chart C. Change to 5mm (US 8) needle, cast off the steek sts and work garter st rows for 4cm (1½in). Cast (bind) off.

In the steek sts, sew two double seams with a sewing machine. You can either cut before picking up sts for the edge, or you can wait until both edges have been knitted. Pick up sts with 5mm (US 8) needle and pattern colour 1 along the right side of the blanket (pick up 2 sts, skip 1 st, rep to end). When you have the correct number of sts on the needle, run a strand of contrasting yarn through all the sts. This makes it easier to pick up sts for the binding to cover the cut edge later on. Work garter st rows for 4cm (1½in). Cast (bind) off. Repeat on the left side.

Binding: Now that there is a strand of contrasting yarn through the sts, it is easy to know which sts to pick up for binding. Using 6mm (US 10) needle and pattern colour 1, pick up sts where the contrasting yarn is (pick up 2, skip 1, rep to end) and then remove the strand. Work 4 rows stocking (stockinette) st. Cast (bind) off and sew the binding loosely over the cut edge. Repeat on the other side. Alternatively, you can hide the cut edge by sewing on a ribbon.

Make fringes using the base colour. See page 168 for details.

Chart C

Chart B

Chart A

TIPI cushion

MEASUREMENTS
60x50cm (23¾x19¾in)

TENSION (GAUGE)
10cm (4in) on 6mm (US 10) needle = 13 sts

YARN
Álafosslopi, Blåne or Troll from Hillesvåg Ullvarefabrikk, or Rauma Vams and one strand Lamullgarn

AMOUNT OF YARN

Base colour: 300g (10½oz)

Pattern colour 1: 100g (3½oz)

Pattern colour 2: 100g (3½oz)

Pattern colour 3: 100g (3½oz)

Pattern colour 4: 100g (3½oz)

KNITTING NEEDLES
6mm (US 10) 80cm or 100cm (32in or 40in) circular needle
5mm (US 8) 80cm (32in) circular needle (for removable cushion cover)

BUTTONS
7 22mm (1in) buttons (for removable cushion cover)

With 6mm (US 10) needle and base colour, cast on 160 sts and place a marker at the beginning of the needle and after 80 sts (one marker on each side). Knit the chart. The cushion is knitted in stocking (stockinette) st in the round. When you have finished the chart, sew together with Kitchener stitch.

Weave in ends. Rinse the cushion and stretch it into shape. Let it dry flat. Fill the cushion (e.g. 60x50cm (23¾x19¾in) inner cushion from Ikea). Sew together the other side.

Removable cushion cover:
If you would like a removable cushion cover, cast (bind) off the first 80 sts (=backside). Change to 5mm (US 8) needle and work the remaining 80 sts in garter st rows for 2cm (¾in). Make 7 buttonholes (knit 2 sts together, yarn over) evenly spaced. Continue in garter st for 2cm (¾in) and cast (bind) off. Sew buttons on backside.

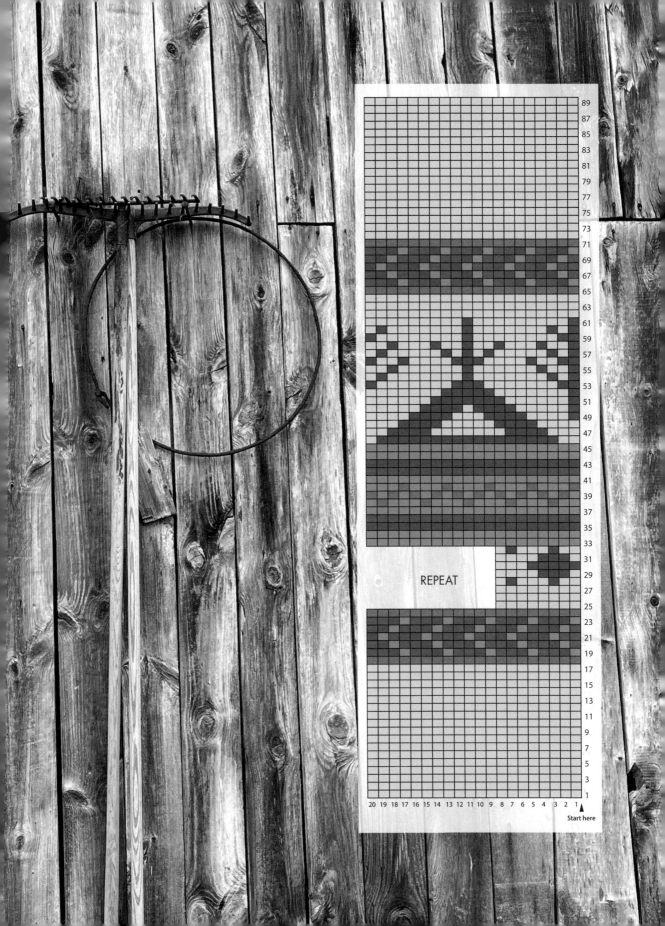

Polarbarn
blankets

I felt like knitting a blanket for my baby when I became pregnant. I wanted to give her a gift from me that she could grow up with and attach good childhood memories to – and maybe even want to use when she has children herself.

The blanket is thick (double) and quite large – it is perfect to use as a hiking blanket, in the pram or over a duvet when it is cold. I have also made a variation that is single-sided and with fewer colours.

POLARBARN blanket

MEASUREMENTS
Length: approx. 121cm (47¾in)
Width: approx. 92cm (36¼in)

TENSION (GAUGE)
10cm (4in) on 5mm (US 8) needle = 17 sts

YARN
Vidde from Hillesvåg Ullvarefabrikk (can be combined with Varde from Hillesvåg Ullvarefabrikk)

AMOUNT OF YARN

- Base colour: 500g (17½oz)
- Edge colour and pattern colour 1: 500g (17½oz)
- Pattern colour 2: 200g (7oz)
- Pattern colour 3: 100g (3½oz)
- Pattern colour 4: 100g (3½oz)
- Pattern colour 5: 100g (3½oz)
- Pattern colour 6: 100g (3½oz)

KNITTING NEEDLES
4.5mm & 5mm (US 7 & 8) 80cm (32in) circular needles

Note! In some places on the back there will be long floats, make sure to catch them as you work.

With 4.5mm (US 7) needle and edge colour, cast on 132 sts. Work garter st rows for 4cm (1½in). Change to 5mm (US 8) needle and cast on 132 sts so that you now have 264 sts on the needle. Insert a marker on each side. Continue in stocking (stockinette) st in the round. Work charts A, B, and C. When you have completed the charts, cast (bind) off the last 132 sts. Change to 4.5mm needle and work garter st over the remaining 132 sts for 4cm (1½in). Cast (bind) off.

The markers on each side indicate where to pick up sts for the garter st edge. One tip is to do a basting stitch before you start picking up sts to make sure the edge is straight. With 4.5mm (US 7) needle and edge colour, pick up sts (pick up 2, skip 1, rep to end) between two rows (so that the blanket looks the same on both sides). Work garter st rows for 7cm (2¾in). Cast (bind) off. Repeat on the other side.

Weave in ends on the inside of the blanket and sew together the top and bottom edges to close the blanket.

This blanket is doubled, and just as nice on both sides. If you want a lighter and simpler version, see the pattern and instructions on pages 110–11.

Chart A

Chart C

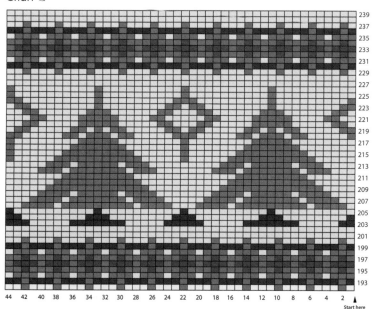

239 237 235 233 231 229 227 225 223 221 219 217 215 213 211 209 207 205 203 201 199 197 195 193

44 42 40 38 36 34 32 30 28 26 24 22 20 18 16 14 12 10 8 6 4 2
Start here

Chart B

191 189 187 185 183 181 179 177 175 173 171 169 167 165 163 161 159 157 155 153 151 149 147 145 143 141 139 137 135 133 131 129 127 125 123 121 119 117 115 113 111 109 107

44 42 40 38 36 34 32 30 28 26 24 22 20 18 16 14 12 10 8 6 4 2
Start here

Vidde
Kamel 69336
Lys oransje 69329
Korall 69312
Brun 69322
Petrolgrønn 69334
Støvet oliven 69337
Lys turkis 69303

POLARBARN single-sided blanket

MEASUREMENTS

Length: approx. 121cm (47¾in)
Width: approx. 92cm (36¼in)

TENSION (GAUGE)

10cm (4in) on 5mm (US 8) needle = 17 sts

YARN

Vidde yarn from Hillesvåg Ullvarefabrikk (can be combined with Varde from Hillesvåg Ullvarefabrikk)

AMOUNT OF YARN

- Base colour: 300g (10½oz)
- Edge colour and pattern colour 1: 300g (10½oz)
- Pattern colour 2: 100g (3½oz)
- Pattern colour 3: 100g (3½oz)
- Pattern colour 4: 100g (3½oz)

KNITTING NEEDLES

4.5mm & 5mm (US 7 & 8) 80cm (32in) circular needles

> Note! In some places on the back there will be long floats, make sure to catch them as you work.

With 4.5mm (US 7) needle and edge colour, cast on 132 sts. Work garter st rows for 4cm (1½in). Cast on 5 sts on right needle for steek sts (these sts are not included in the number of sts and are worked purl at all times.) From here, work stocking (stockinette) st in the round. Change to 5mm (US 8) needle and work charts A, B, and C.

When you have finished the charts, knit 1 round in edge colour and cast (bind) off the steek sts. Change to 4.5mm (US 7) needle and work garter st rows for 4cm (1½in). Cast (bind) off.

In the steek sts, sew two double seams with a sewing machine. You can either cut before picking up sts for the edge, or you can wait until both edges have been knitted. Using 4.5mm (US 7) needle and edge colour, pick up sts along the right side of the blanket (pick up 2 sts, skip 1 st, rep to end). When all the sts are on the needle, run a strand of contrasting yarn through all the sts. This makes it easier to pick up sts for the binding to cover the cut edge later on. Work garter st rows for 7cm (3¾in). Cast (bind) off. Repeat on the left side.

Binding: Now that there is a strand of contrasting yarn through the sts, it is easy to know which sts to pick up for the binding. Using 5mm (US 8) needle and base colour, pick up sts where the contrasting yarn is (pick up 2, skip 1, rep to end) and then remove the strand. Work 4 rows in stocking (stockinette) st. Cast (bind) off and sew the binding loosely over the cut edge. Repeat on the other side. Alternatively, you can hide the cut edge by sewing on a ribbon.

Weave in ends. Rinse the blanket and stretch it into shape. Let it dry flat.

Chart A

Chart C

Chart B

Elise's
tapestry

I designed this tapestry with Elise, my five-year-old niece.
She loves unicorns and princesses. Elise knew exactly
what the unicorn should look like. The unicorn is on its hind
legs and the mane and tail should have many colours. I
approached it by first knitting the unicorn in one colour, and
then I went over with Swiss darning (duplicate stitch) and
used yarn in different colours. My exacting niece thankfully
approved the end result, and now the tapestry is hanging in
her room.

Troll
Mintgrønn 02748
Lys gul 02709
Lillarosa 02721
Lilla 02750
Marineblå 02724
Halvbleket hvit 02754
Sukkerspinn 02753

ELISE'S tapestry

MEASUREMENTS
Height: approx. 77cm (30¼in) without fringe
Width: approx. 62cm (24½in)

TENSION (GAUGE)
10cm (4in) on 6mm (US 10) needle = 13 sts

YARN
Álafosslopi, Blåne or Troll from Hillesvåg Ullvarefabrikk, or Rauma Vams and one strand Lamullgarn

AMOUNT OF YARN
- Pattern colour 1: 200g (7oz)
- Pattern colour 2: 200g (7oz)
- Pattern colour 3: 200g (7oz)
- Pattern colour 4: 200g (7oz)
- Pattern colour 5: 200g (7oz)
- Pattern colour 6: 200g (7oz)
- Additional colour for embroidery on mane and tail

TOOLS
6mm (US 10) 60cm (24in) circular needle
Crochet hook for the fringe
Wool needle
Wooden stick for hanging
Sewing machine

With 6mm (US 10) needle and pattern colour 1, cast on 73 sts. Work garter st rows for 4cm (1½in). Cast on 5 sts on right needle for steek sts (these sts are not included in the number of sts and are worked purl at all times). From here, work in stocking (stockinette) st in the round. Work chart A. When the chart is completed, work garter st in pattern colour 1 for 12cm (4¾in) (this will become the rod sleeve). Cast (bind) off.

In the steek sts, sew two double seams with a sewing machine. You can either cut before picking up sts for the edge, or you can wait until both edges have been knitted. Pick up sts in pattern colour 5 along the right edge of the tapestry (pick up 2 sts, skip 1 st, rep to end). Work garter st rows for 3cm (1¼in). Cast (bind) off. Repeat on the left side.

Trim the cut edges. Do not knit binding to hide the cut edge, as it will appear on the front of the tapestry. You can hide the cut edge by sewing on a ribbon.

Use Swiss darning (duplicate stitch) to embroider the colourful mane and tail in chart B.

Make fringe with pattern colour 5. See page 168 for details. Weave in ends. Rinse the tapestry and stretch it into shape. Let it dry flat.

Fold over the rod sleeve and sew it to the tapestry. Insert the wooden stick. See page 168 for details.

> Note! In some places on the back there will be long floats, make sure to catch them as you work.

Chart A

104
102
100
98
96
94
92
90
88
86
84
82
80
78
76
74
72
70
68
66
64
62
60
58
56
54
52
50
48
46
44
42
40
38
36
34
32
30
28
26
24
22
20
18
16
14
12
10
8
6
4
2

73 71 69 67 65 63 61 59 57 55 53 51 49 47 45 43 41 39 37 35 33 31 29 27 25 23 21 19 17 15 13 11 9 7 5 3 1

Start here

Chart B

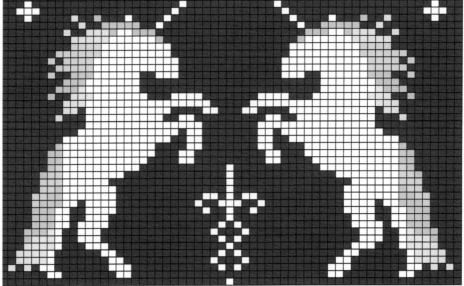

This chart shows where you embroider with Swiss darning (duplicate stitch) to make a colourful mane and tail. Learn how online, e.g. at www.garnstudio.com.

Álafosslopi and Léttlopi
Black tweed 809975
Léttlopi held double: Rust heather 19427
Oatmeal heather 800085
Acorn heather 800053
Light ash heather 800054
Dark olive 809987

Alasuq sweater
(Pattern in *Wilderness Knits*)

Álafosslopi
Black tweed 809975
Highland green 801230
Teal heather 809967
Ash heather 800056
Léttlopi held double: Rust heather 19427

Føyka cushion

The Føyka pattern is from my first book. This is perhaps the pattern that is knitted in the most colour combinations. See #føykagenser on Instagram for inspiration.

Troll and Blåne
Blåne Cognac 672103
Troll Melert oransje 027011
Blåne Rødgul 672122

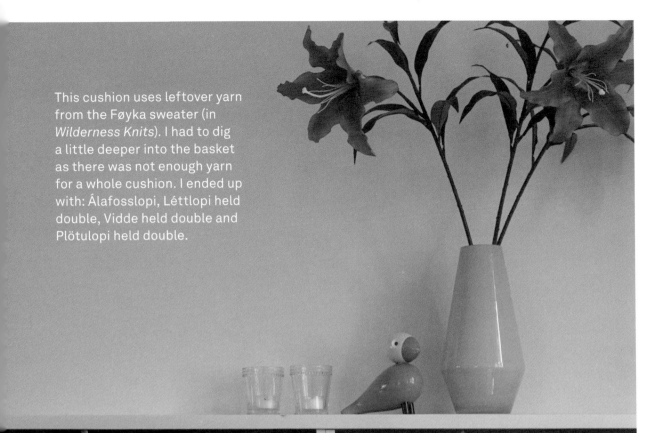

This cushion uses leftover yarn from the Føyka sweater (in *Wilderness Knits*). I had to dig a little deeper into the basket as there was not enough yarn for a whole cushion. I ended up with: Álafosslopi, Léttlopi held double, Vidde held double and Plötulopi held double.

FØYKA cushion

MEASUREMENTS

60x50cm (23¾x19¾in)

TENSION (GAUGE)

10cm (4in) on 6mm (US 10) needle = 13 sts

YARN

Álafosslopi, Blåne or Troll from Hillesvåg Ullvarefabrikk, or Rauma Vams and one strand Lamullgarn

AMOUNT OF YARN

Base colour: 300g (10½oz)

Pattern colour 1: 200g (7oz)

Pattern colour 2: 100g (3½oz)

KNITTING NEEDLES

6mm (US 10) 80cm or 100cm (32in or 40in) circular needle
5mm (US 8) 80cm (32in) circular needle (for removable cushion cover)

BUTTONS

7 22mm (1in) buttons (for removable cushion cover)

With 6mm (US 10) needle and base colour, cast on 156 sts and place a marker at the beginning of the needle and after 78 sts (one marker on each side). Work the chart. The cushion is knitted in stocking (stockinette) st in the round. When you have finished the chart, sew together with Kitchener stitch.

Weave in ends. Rinse the cushion and stretch it into shape. Let it dry flat. Fill the cushion (e.g. 60x50cm (23¾x19¾in) inner cushion from Ikea). Sew together the other side.

Removable cushion cover:
If you would like a removable cushion cover, cast (bind) off the first 78 sts (=backside). Change to 5mm (US 8) needle and work the remaining 78 sts in garter st rows for 2cm (¾in). Make 7 buttonholes (knit 2 sts together, yarn over) evenly spaced. Continue in garter st for 2cm (¾in) and cast (bind) off. Sew buttons on backside.

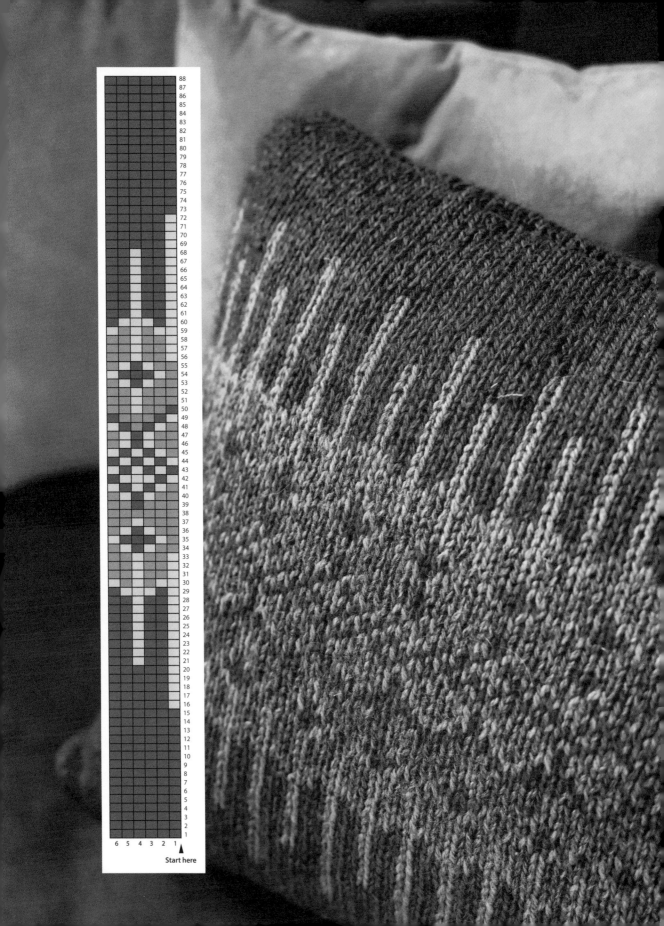

88
87
86
85
84
83
82
81
80
79
78
77
76
75
74
73
72
71
70
69
68
67
66
65
64
63
62
61
60
59
58
57
56
55
54
53
52
51
50
49
48
47
46
45
44
43
42
41
40
39
38
37
36
35
34
33
32
31
30
29
28
27
26
25
24
23
22
21
20
19
18
17
16
15
14
13
12
11
10
9
8
7
6
5
4
3
2
1

6 5 4 3 2 1
▲
Start here

Troll and Blåne
Troll Melert pudderrosa 027331
Troll Melert lys blåturkis 027060
Blåne Petrol 672105
Troll Ubleket hvit 02702
Troll Mørk kamel 02714

Keiko cushion

I have always been fascinated by orcas. When I asked my sister and mother if they wanted to test knit for the book, both chose the Keiko cushion! We now have one in each of our homes, and one at our family home in Lista.

Troll
Bonderød 02746
Melert oransje 027011
Svart 02708
Ubleket hvit 02702
Lys blåturkis 02760

SVARTULV CUSHION (p.138)

TAKOTNA CUSHION (p.74)

Troll
Oker 02713
Melert lys blåturkis 027060
Mintgrønn 02748
Blek fersken 02743
Svart 02708

UMA CUSHION (p.88)

KEIKO cushion

MEASUREMENTS

50x50cm (19¾x19¾)

TENSION (GAUGE)

10cm (4in) on 5.5mm (US 9) needle
= 14 sts

YARN

Álafosslopi, Blåne or Troll from Hillesvåg
Ullvarefabrikk, or Rauma Vams and one
strand Lamullgarn

AMOUNT OF YARN

Base colour 1: 200g (7oz)

Base colour 2: 200g (7oz)

Pattern colour 1: 200g (7oz)

Pattern colour 2: 100g (3½oz)

Pattern colour 3: 100g (3½oz)

KNITTING NEEDLES

5.5mm (US 9) 80cm (32in) circular needle
4.5mm (US 7) 80cm (32in) circular
needles (for removable cushion cover)

BUTTONS

6 22mm (1in) buttons (for removable
cushion cover)

With 5.5mm (US 9) needle and base colour 1, cast on
144 sts and place a marker at the beginning of the
needle and after 72 sts (one marker on each side).
Work the chart. The cushion is knitted in stocking
(stockinette) st in the round. When you have finished
the chart, sew together with Kitchener stitch.

Weave in ends. Rinse the cushion and stretch it into
shape. Let it dry flat. Fill the cushion (e.g. 50x50cm
(19¾x19¾) inner cushion from Ikea). Sew together
the other side.

Removable cushion cover:
If you would like a removable cushion cover, cast
(bind) off the first 72 sts (=backside). Change to
4.5mm (US 7) needle and work the remaining 72 sts
in garter st rows for 2cm (¾in). Make 6 buttonholes
(knit 2 sts together, yarn over) evenly spaced.
Continue for 2cm (¾in) and cast (bind) off. Sew
buttons on backside.

> Note! In some places on the back
> there will be long floats, make sure
> to catch them as you work.

Troll and Blåne
Troll Oker 02713
Troll Kobberrød 02716
Blåne Turkis 672106
Blåne Rød 672132
Blåne Ren grønn 672141

Solskog cushion

The winter was about to end and I looked forward
to long, bright summer nights. That was what
inspired me to create this cushion.

Troll and Álafosslopi
Troll Oker 02713
Troll Lys blåturkis 02760
Troll Melert petrolgrønn 027334
Troll Melert rustrød 027308
Álafosslopi Black tweed 809975

SOLSKOG cushion

MEASUREMENTS

60x50cm (23¾x19¾in)

TENSION (GAUGE)

10cm (4in) on 6mm (US 10) needle = 13 sts

YARN

Álafosslopi, Blåne or Troll from Hillesvåg Ullvarefabrikk, or Rauma Vams and one strand Lamullgarn

AMOUNT OF YARN

Base colour 1: 200g (7oz)

Base colour 2: 200g (7oz)

Pattern colour 1: 100g (3½oz)

Pattern colour 2: 100g (3½oz)

Pattern colour 3: 100g (3½oz)

KNITTING NEEDLES

6mm (US 10) 80cm (32in) circular needle
5mm (US 8) 80cm (32in) circular needle
(for removable cushion cover)

BUTTONS

7 22mm (1in) buttons (for removable cushion cover)

With 6mm (US 10) needle and base colour 1, cast on 150 sts and place a marker at the beginning of the needle and after 75 sts (one marker on each side). Work the chart. The cushion is knitted in stocking (stockinette) st in the round. When you have finished the chart, sew together with Kitchener stitch.

Weave in ends. Rinse the cushion and stretch it into shape. Let it dry flat. Fill the cushion (e.g. 60x50cm (23¾x19¾in) inner cushion from Ikea). Sew together the other side.

Removable cushion cover:
If you would like a removable cushion cover, cast (bind) off the first 75 sts (=backside). Change to 5mm (US 8)needle and work the remaining 75 sts in garter st rows for 2cm (¾in). Make 7 buttonholes (knit 2 sts together, yarn over) evenly spaced. Continue for 2cm (¾in) and cast (bind) off. Sew buttons on backside.

SVARTULV cushion

MEASUREMENTS
50x50cm (19¾x19¾in)

TENSION (GAUGE)
10cm (4in) on 5.5mm (US 9) needle
= 14 sts

YARN
Álafosslopi, Blåne or Troll from Hillesvåg
Ullvarefabrikk, or Rauma Vams and one
strand Lamullgarn

AMOUNT OF YARN
☐ Base colour: 300g (10½oz)

■ Pattern colour 1: 200g (7oz)

KNITTING NEEDLES
5.5mm (US 9) 80cm (32in) circular needle
4.5mm (US 7) 80cm (32in) circular needle
(for removable cushion cover)

BUTTONS
6 22mm (1in) buttons (for removable
cushion cover)

With 5.5mm (US 9) needle and base colour, cast on
140 sts and place a marker at the beginning of the
needle and after 70 sts (one marker on each side).
Work the chart. The cushion is knitted in stocking
(stockinette) st in the round. When you have finished
the chart, sew together with Kitchener stitch.

Weave in the ends. Rinse the cushion and stretch
it into shape. Let it dry flat. Fill the cushion (e.g.
50x50cm (19¾x19¾in) inner cushion from Ikea).
Sew together the other side.

Removable cushion cover:
If you would like a removable cushion cover, cast
(bind) off the first 70 sts (=backside). Change to
4.5mm (US 7) needle and work the remaining 70 sts
in garter st rows for 2cm (¾in). Make 6 buttonholes
(knit 2 sts together, yarn over) evenly spaced.
Continue for 2cm (¾in) and cast (bind) off. Sew
buttons on backside.

Alafosslopi
Light beige heather 800086
Dark olive 809987

Troll
Melert lys brun 02705
Brun 02715
Bonderød 02746
Lys blåturkis 02760
Svart 02708
Melert oransje 027011

Tundra
cushion

When I design, I always look for contrasts and
contexts, and things around me for inspiration.
A belt I received from my father, which he used
when he was a child, inspired the pattern borders
on this cushion. The belt is hanging in our dining
room because I think it is so decorative.

Troll and Blåne
Troll Melert lys brun 02705
Blåne Olivengrønn 672118
Blåne Støvet rosa 672137
Troll Melert oransje 027011
Blåne Petrol 672105
Troll Isblå 02745

TUNDRA cushion

MEASUREMENTS
50x50cm (19¾x19¾in)

TENSION (GAUGE)
10cm (4in) on 6mm (US 10) needle = 13 sts

YARN
Álafosslopi, Blåne or Troll from Hillesvåg Ullvarefabrikk, or Rauma Vams and one strand Lamullgarn

AMOUNT OF YARN

☐ Base colour: 200g (7oz)

■ Pattern colour 1: 100g (3½oz)

■ Pattern colour 2: 100g (3½oz)

☐ Pattern colour 3: 100g (3½oz)

■ Pattern colour 4: 100g (3½oz)

☐ Pattern colour 5: 100g (3½oz)

Feel free to use leftover yarn for pattern colour 3 and 5 as you will only use a small amount.

KNITTING NEEDLES
6mm (US 10) 80cm (32in) circular needle
5mm (US 8) 80cm (32in) circular needle (for removable cushion cover)

BUTTONS
6 22mm (1in) buttons (for removable cushion cover)

With 6mm (US 10) needle and base colour, cast on 132 sts and place a marker at the beginning of the needle and after 66 sts (one marker on each side). Work the chart. The cushion is knitted in stocking (stockinette) st in the round. When you have finished the chart, sew together with Kitchener stitch.

Weave in ends. Rinse the cushion and stretch it into shape. Let it dry flat. Fill the cushion (e.g. 50x50cm (19¾x19¾in) inner cushion from Ikea). Sew together the other side.

Removable cushion cover:
If you would like a removable cushion cover, cast (bind) off the first 66 sts (=backside). Change to 5mm (US 8) needle and work the remaining 66 sts in garter st rows for 2cm (¾in). Make 6 buttonholes (knit 2 sts together, yarn over) evenly spaced. Continue for 2cm (¾in) and cast (bind) off. Sew buttons on backside.

> Note! In some places on the back there will be long floats, make sure to catch them as you work.

Troll
Melert petrolgrønn 027334
Marineblå 02724
Ubleket hvit 02702
Melert lys korall 027318
Oker 02713
Melert rustrød 027308

Lista cushion

Álafosslopi
Acorn heather 800053
Ash heather 800056
Ecru heather 809972
Sheep sorrel 801237
Dark olive 809987
Chartreuse green heather 809965

LISTA cushion

MEASUREMENTS
60x50cm (23¾x19¾in)

TENSION (GAUGE)
10cm (4in) on 6mm (US 10) needle = 13 sts

YARN
Álafosslopi, Blåne or Troll from Hillesvåg Ullvarefabrikk, or Rauma Vams and one strand Lamullgarn

AMOUNT OF YARN

Base colour 1: Troll/Blåne: 100g (3½oz) / Álafosslopi: 200g (7oz)

Base colour 2: Troll/Blåne: 100g (3½oz) / Álafosslopi: 200g (7oz)

Pattern colour 1: 100g (3½oz)

Pattern colour 2: 100g (3½oz)

Pattern colour 3: 100g (3½oz)

Pattern colour 4: 100g (3½oz)

KNITTING NEEDLES
6mm (US 10) 80cm or 100cm (32in or 40in) circular needle
5mm (US 8) 80cm (32in) circular needle (for removable cushion cover)

BUTTONS
7 22mm (1in) buttons (for removable cushion cover)

With 6mm (US 10) needle and base colour 1, cast on 160 sts and place a marker at the beginning of the needle and after 80 sts (one marker on each side). Work the chart. The cushion is knitted in stocking (stockinette) st in the round. When you have finished the chart, sew together with Kitchener stitch.

Weave in loose ends. Rinse the cushion and stretch it into shape. Let it dry flat. Fill the cushion (e.g. 60x50cm (23¾x19¾in) inner cushion from Ikea). Sew together the other side.

Removable cushion cover:
If you would like a removable cushion cover, cast off the first 80 sts (=backside). Change to 5mm (US 8) needle and work the remaining 80 sts in garter st rows for 2cm (¾in). Make 7 buttonholes (knit 2 sts together, yarn over) evenly spaced. Continue for 2cm (¾in) and cast (bind) off. Sew buttons on backside.

Troll
Melert petrolgrønn 027334
Marineblå 02724
Ubleket hvit 02702
Melert lys korall 027318
Oker 02713
Melert rustrød 027308

Start here

Vams
Mosegrønn melert 406
Mosegrønn 86
Terrakotta 42
Mørk brun melert 64

Åsgreina blanket

The Åsgreina blanket is named after the place I live. It was my first design in a new house. I started knitting the blanket on a long road trip to Lofoten. I find it boring to make single-coloured things, so I knitted with double yarn in two different shades of the same colour to make it a little more exciting. I knitted and knitted and knitted. It felt like a training session to knit such a large blanket, but in the end I finished! And it was worth it. The blanket is big and lovely, and we use it a lot.

ÅSGREINA blanket

MEASUREMENTS

Size: M(L)
Length: approx. 160(210)cm (63(82½)in)
Width: approx. 117(157)cm (46(61¾)in)

TENSION (GAUGE)

10cm (4in) on 10mm (US 15) needle
= 9 sts

YARN

Rauma Vams in two shades held double

AMOUNT OF YARN

Base colour 1: 700(1000)g (24½(35¼)oz)
Base colour 2: 700(1000)g (24½(35¼)oz)
Fringe colour 1: 50(100)g (1¾(3½)oz)
Fringe colour 2: 50(100)g (1¾(3½)oz)

TOOLS

10mm (US 15) circular needle
Crochet hook for the fringes

The blanket is knitted in rows with yarn held double (base colour 1 and 2).

Part 1

With 10mm (US 15) needle and base colour 1 and 2 held together, cast on 106(142) sts. Knit 3 rows knit sts so that two garter st ridges are visible on the right side of the blanket. Then work rib (purl 2 sts, knit 2 sts, rep to end) for 6cm (2¼in). The last row of the rib should be on the right side of the blanket. Finish off by knitting 3 rows knit sts (you will then get two visible garter st ridges on the right side of the blanket).

Main part

From here knit 6 sts at the beginning and end of each row for garter st edge. Work stocking (stockinette) st rows for 12cm (4¾in) and finish with 1 knit row. Continue knitting 3 rows in knit sts, so that two garter st ridges are visible on the right side of the blanket. Repeat until the blanket measures approx. 150(200)cm (59(78¾in). Finish off by knitting 3 rows in knit sts (you will then get two visible garter st ridges on the right side of the blanket). Work part 3.

Part 3

Work rib (purl 2 sts, knit 2 sts, rep to end) for 6cm (2¼in). The last row of rib should be on the right side of the blanket. Finish by knitting 3 rows in knit sts (then you will get two visible garter st ridges on the right side of the blanket). Cast (bind) off.

Fringes

Make fringes in fringe colour 1 and 2. See page 168 for details. Weave in ends. Rinse the blanket and stretch it into shape. Let it dry flat.

Vams
Beige melert 06
Kamel 63
Lys gråblå 110
Rød melert 400

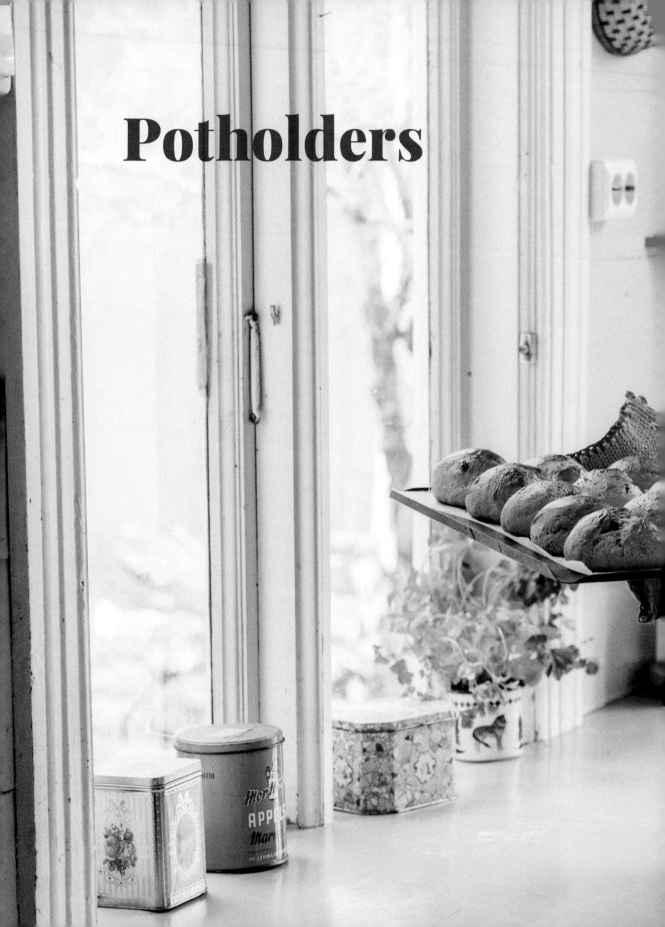

Potholders

Sumatra cotton yarn
Mørk jeansblå 3062
Sjøgrønn 3017
Rustrød 3052
Mørk gul 3077
Hvit 3003

Sumatra cotton yarn
Sjøgrønn 3017
Kamelbrun 3074
Mørk oransje 3059
Sennepsgul 3050

Sumatra cotton yarn
Rustrød 3052
Rødbrun 3073
Skogsgrønn 3078
Sennepsgul 3050
Mørk lilla 3031

Rustrød 3052
Rødbrun 3073
Skogsgrønn 3078
Sennepsgul 3050
Mørk lilla 3031
Blå 3294

AUTUMN potholders

MEASUREMENTS

Height: 21cm (8¼in) including crochet edge
Length: 23cm (9in) including crochet edge

TENSION (GAUGE)

10cm (4in) on 4.5mm (US 7) needle = 18 sts

YARN

Sumatra cotton yarn from Rauma

AMOUNT OF YARN
(potholders 1 & 2)

Base colour: 50g (1¾oz)
Pattern colour 1: 50g (1¾oz)
Pattern colour 2: 50g (1¾oz)
Pattern colour 3: 50g (1¾oz)
Pattern colour 4: 50g (1¾oz)

AMOUNT OF YARN
(potholder 3)

Base colour: 50g (1¾oz)
Pattern colour 1: 50g (1¾oz)
Pattern colour 2: 50g (1¾oz)
Pattern colour 3: 50g (1¾oz)
Pattern colour 4: 50g (1¾oz)
Pattern colour 5: 50g (1¾oz)

TOOLS

4.5mm (US 7) 40cm (16in) circular needle
4.5mm (US G) crochet hook for edge

The potholders are double thickness and knitted in the round. With 4.5mm needle cast on 80 sts. Place a marker in each side before sts 1 and 41. Work chart and cast (bind) off. Weave in ends.

Crochet edges: The markers on each side indicate where to pick up sts for the crochet edge. To close top and bottom of the potholder, sts are worked through both layers. With 4.5mm (US G) hook, work a double (single) crochet edge around the entire potholder.

Hanging loop: Chain 9 sts and attach the loop to the crochet edge.

If you do not want a crochet edge, you can sew together top and bottom and use a small leather cord as a loop. Remember to remove the leather cord before washing.

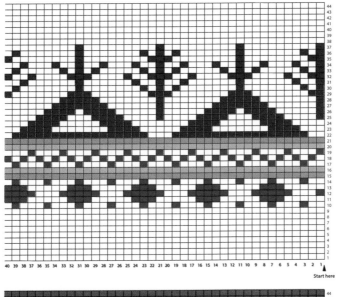

Potholder 1

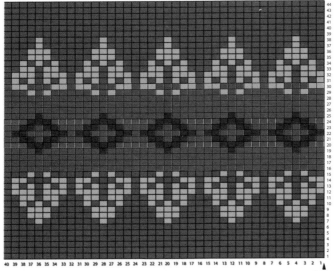

Potholder 2

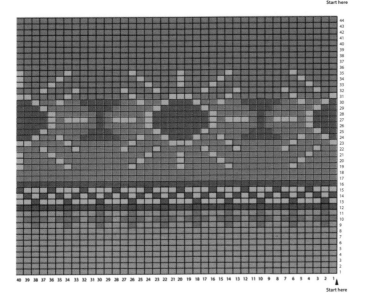

Potholder 3

165

SUMMER potholders

MEASUREMENTS

Height: 21cm (8¼in) including crochet
edge
Length: 23cm (9in) including crochet
edge

TENSION (GAUGE)

10cm (4in) on 4.5mm (US 7) needle
= 18 sts

YARN

Sumatra cotton yarn from Rauma

AMOUNT OF YARN

Base colour: 50g (1¾oz)
Pattern colour 1: 50g (1¾oz)
Pattern colour 2: 50g (1¾oz)
Pattern colour 3: 50g (1¾oz)

TOOLS

4.5mm (US 7) 40cm (16in) circular needle
4.5mm (US G) crochet hook for edge

The potholders are double thickness and knitted
in the round. With 4.5mm (US 7) needle cast on
72 sts. Place a marker on each side before sts 1 and
37. Work chart and cast (bind) off. Weave in ends.

Crochet edge: The markers on each side indicate
where to pick up sts for the crochet edge. To close
top and bottom of the potholder, sts are worked
through both layers. With 4.5mm (US G) hook,
work a double (single) crochet edge around the
entire potholder.

Hanging loop: Chain 9 sts and attach the loop to
the crochet edge.

If you do not want a crochet edge, you can sew
together top and bottom and use a small leather
cord as a loop. Remember to remove the cord
before washing.

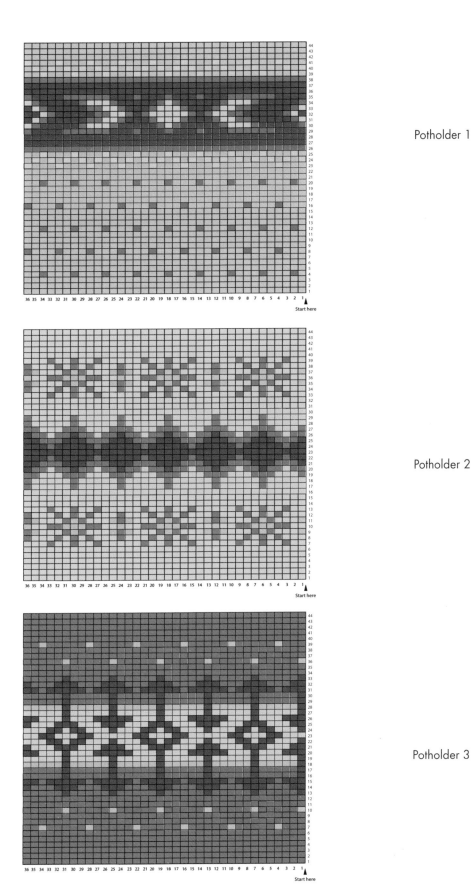

Potholder 1

Potholder 2

Potholder 3

Hanging tapestries

For hanging, you can use an old rod, stick, or a wooden dowel that you will need to saw to the desired length.

Fringes

Cut threads measuring 28cm (11in). Fold 2 strands double so that each fringe has 4 ends. Insert a crochet hook through the edge of the work and pull the doubled yarn through so that there is a large loop. Pull the end of the yarn through this loop and tighten. Place on every other stitch. When the fringes are completed, they can be trimmed to the same length.

Assembling tapestries & blankets

You can either sew with a machine before picking up stitches for the edge, or you can wait until both edges have been knitted. I prefer the latter, as the knitting is then firmer and easier to work with. Pick up stitches along the right side of the blanket, and feel free to use a crochet hook (pick up 2 sts, skip 1 st, rep to end).

When all the stitches are on the needle, thread a strand of contrasting yarn through all the stitches. This makes it easier to pick up stitches for the binding to cover the cut edge later.

Knit edge.
Repeat on the other side.

Sew two double stitches with a sewing machine in the steek stitches. Cut between the seams.

Now that there is a strand of contrasting yarn through the stitches, it is easy to know which stitches to pick up for the binding. Pick up stitches where the contrasting yarn is located, and then remove the strand. Work 4 rows stocking (stockinette) st. Cast (bind) off and sew the binding loosely over the cut edge.

Repeat on the other side. Alternatively, you can hide the cut edge by sewing on a ribbon.

Stitching cushions together

It is prettiest if you stitch together at the top. There are many simple descriptions online.

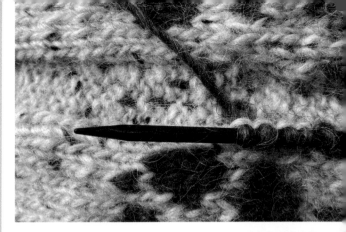
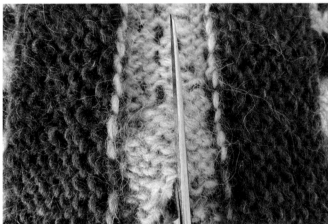

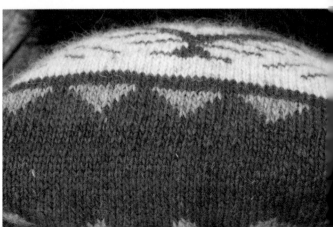

Thank you

Many thanks to everyone who has been part of the team and made this project possible! Thanks to my test knitters, and especially Bente Martinsen, who has knitted almost every pattern in this book. Thanks to Stine and Halvdan, who have once again done an incredible job with the photography. A big thank you to my team at Aschehoug, Kitty and Sirikit! And not least a big thank you to Hillesvåg Ullvarefabrikk and Rauma Yarn who have contributed with yarn.

And finally a big thank you to Waqas, who always has faith in me and my projects <3